Applied Psychology

Volume 9

MIND

MASTERY

Being the Ninth of a Series of Twelve Volumes on the Applications of Psychology to the Problems of Personal and Business Efficiency

BY

WARREN HILTON, A.B., L.L.B.

FOUNDER OF THE SOCIETY OF APPLIED PSYCHOLOGY

**ISSUED UNDER THE AUSPICES OF
THE LITERARY DIGEST
FOR
NEW YORK AND LONDON
1919**

**Republished from the public domain
by**

Creative English Publishing

www.Creative-English-Institute.com

Under Classic Reads

May 2014

**ISBN-13:
978-1499592481**

**ISBN-10:
1499592485**

CONTENTS

CONSCIOUS DOMINANCE OF SELF AND THINGS

Chapter IX. page 87
SCIENTIFIC EXPLANATION OF HYPNOTISM

MENTAL EQUILIBRIUM AND POWERS OF RESISTANCE

CONTROLLING SUBJECTS AT A DISTANCE

HYPNOSIS DISTINGUISHED FROM NATURAL SLEEP

THE MENTAL PROCESS THAT EXPLAINS HYPNOTISM

THE STATE OF ABNORMAL CONCENTRATION

PRACTICAL ASPECTS OF MIND CONTROL

Chapter I

PRACTICAL ASPECTS OF MIND CONTROL

CORAL ISLANDS AND SUNLIT SEAS

CORAL island is composed of the cemented bodies of its tiny builders. It shows but little above the surface of the sea. There is a lake of iridescent green. There is an encircling ring of tropic vegetation. There are foaming breakers and gleaming sands. But in all you see you will find no hint of that mighty supporting structure that has its base in unfathomable depths and rises to the sun. Your mind is like this coral island.

THE GERM OF ACHIEVEMENT

It is built of the associated sense-impressions of all past experience. Just now, certain perceptions, emotions, impulses and ideas are scintillating in the sun of consciousness. Beneath the surface in the unlit sea of the subconscious is the mind that prompts the heartthrob and the breath — the mind of stored-up memories and powers, the mind that holds within itself the germ of all present achievement.

Considered from the standpoint of its activities, the subconscious is that department of mind, which on the one hand directs the vital operations of the body, and on the other conserves, subject to the call of interest and attention, all ideas and complexes not at the moment active in consciousness.

THREE GOALS THIS COURSE LEADS TO

Observe, then, the possibility that lies before you. On the one hand, if you can control your mind in its subconscious activities, you can regulate the operation of your bodily functions, and can thus assure yourself of bodily efficiency and free yourself of functional disease. On the other hand, if you can determine just what ideas shall be brought forth from sub consiousness into consciousness, you can thus select the materials out of which will be woven your conscious judgments, your decisions and your emotional attitudes.

To achieve control of your mind is, then, to attain (a) health, (b) success, and (c) happiness, conditioned only by the circumstances of your environment and the extent and character of your native abilities.

WAY TO BODILY EFFICIENCY

a. Health — not that the devouring ravages of invading bacteria can be rendered harmless or that the normal performance of bodily functions can be restored where the parts have been actually consumed or destroyed, but that, given the necessary food supplies, the organs of your body, from brain to digestive tracts, can through subconscious control be made to do their work with regularity and efficiency; that delusions, obsessions, bad habits, moral perversions and similar disorders can be eliminated; and the bodily operations, from the pulsation of the heart to the intestinal processes and the repair of tissue, can be made so automatically perfect as to leave you free to pursue the nobler ends of life without the distraction of physical discomfort.

SUCCESS AND CONSCIOUS IDEAS

b. Success — because business success, success in any practical pursuit, is a triumph of consciousness. It is a triumph of consciousness in that it is the realization of your conscious ideals through the mastery of your own forces.

Consciousness is the mind of analysis, reason and decision. Consciousness is the mind that controls your active intercourse with the world about you.

Consciousness is more than a mere succession of sensations, feelings, images and desires. Consciousness is purposive, sets a goal and strives to reach it.

CO-ORDINATION OF MENTAL FORCES

Find but the way to determine at will the content of your consciousness, selecting such materials as will aid your purpose, rejecting all that will oppose it, and from that moment you will be able to determine in advance just what your decisions will be under all circumstances, through just what outlet your mental energy shall find release in action. You will be able to marshal your resources, to co-ordinate your powers, to enter the field with new and coordinate energies, and to grasp the full measure of attainment.

SCIENCE OF BEING HAPPY

c. Happiness — for happiness is a mental setting. It is the pleasing emotional state that accompanies the realization of desire.

Now, the realization of desire that produces happiness is not outward physical realization. It is mental realization. There is no joy in the realization of a desire unless you know about it. It is the knowledge, the mental state, that awakens pleasurable emotions. It is the mental image of the thing you want pictured as a present reality that really gives you pleasure. Contrary to the words of the song, "Things are always what they seem."

The world for each one of us is not the sum total of sense-impressions, because most of these are ignored. It is not even the sum total of sense-perceptions, because present sense-perceptions constitute but a small part of the content of consciousness. The world is a play and the mind its only stage. And whether it be tragedy or comedy depends upon what ideas are thrust forward into consciousness to form the cast.

Happiness is thus dependent upon the character of the content of consciousness, dependent upon whether the ideas thrust forth into consciousness from sub consciousness are ideas of grief or joy, depressing or sprightly.

EFFICIENCY'S MAGIC WAND

In this course we place within your grasp the magic wand that will enable you to predetermine the content of your own consciousness. With it you may, if you will, without effort and without strain, live a truly efficient life, and reap as you go along its rich reward, a contented spirit.

CONSCIOUS CONTROL OF VITAL FUNCTIONS

The question will at once suggest itself. How can the mind in its subconscious activities, the phase of the mind that controls the operation of bodily-functions, be itself controlled by the passing momentary consciousness? The answer to this question lies in the nature of the relation between mind and body. In subconsciously directing the conduct of the vital processes, your mind is dealing with your body as part of an organic world. Your body maintains itself upon supplies drawn from the world of matter. It converts that which is nourishing into tissue; it discards the waste. It has to be preserved against such destructive external agencies as tempest, fire and pestilence. The food you eat, the air you breathe, the physical obstacles that you encounter, all directly affect your body and must be taken into account by the subconscious in its management of your bodily mechanism.

But how can the subconscious take these things into account? It has no means of direct communication with the outer world.

And just here lies the answer. Being incapable of direct communication with the outer world the subconscious phases of the mind are dependent upon consciousness for the information necessary to the performance of subconscious bodily functions.

Deliberately determine the make-up of your consciousness, and you can thereby control your bodily activities.

RUNNING THE GAUNTLET OF SELF-INTEREST

All impressions from the external world must first run the gauntlet of the attention as predetermined by the interests of consciousness. Those that are required for present use or are related to your present purposive life are momentarily active in consciousness. All others without inspection are sidetracked into the subconscious warehouse.

All the special senses, such as sight, touch, hearing, and so on, operate through the cerebro-spinal nervous system, the organ of consciousness, and they are our only sources of information as to the external world.

All the mental energy within the countless living cells of the body is therefore dependent for release upon such messages from without as are sent that way by the selective process of attention.

INTERPRETATIVE MEDIUM OF CONSCIOUSNESS

Now, attention is an element or agent of consciousness. It is the instrument employed by consciousness in the discrimination and emphasis of sense-impressions. Attention is the interpretative medium. Attention lays stress upon some, discards others.

Here, then, we have the crux of the whole matter. Your subconscious control of bodily processes is exercised in accordance with such sensory images as are emphasized by your conscious attention. And the greater the concentration of your attention upon any idea, the more exclusively it is dwelt upon in consciousness, the greater will be its power to influence the subconscious control of your bodily mechanism.

CONSCIOUS DOMINANCE OF SELF AND THING

The realization of both material success and a cheerful mental attitude through the conscious control of the attention is possible of accomplishment in much the same way.

We have pointed out that both are dependent upon the content of consciousness. Now, what is it that shapes the content of consciousness from one moment to the next? It is that same selective agency of attention.

Every sense-impression, every idea in consciousness, is linked by association with a multitude of others stored in sub consciousness. It is the attention that singles out one associated idea from among them all for immediate reproduction in consciousness. It is the attention that thus fashions the framework of passing states of consciousness and so establishes the premises from which our mature conclusions are deduced. It is the attention that thus prescribes the mental attitude.

Attention is the basic element in any law of mental control.

BASIC ELEMENT OF MIND CONTROL

Chapter II

BASIC ELEMENT OF MIND CONTROL

THE MENTAL SWITCHBOARD AND HOW IT WORKS

IT WOULD be idle for us to work with elements that we do not understand. What, then, is attention, and how does it operate?

We have referred to attention as a "selective agency," a "discriminatory- process," " a watchful sentinel alert to guard consciousness from all sensory- stimuli (past or present), not bearing the countersign of relevancy." In other words, you know what attention does; but the question is, How does it do it?

What is the mechanism by which attention can cause one sense-perception, one idea, the one attended to, to stand out in clear perspective, while all other sense-perceptions and ideas, or, more accurately, all conflicting sense-impressions and ideas, are ignored?

It is a fundamental fact recognized by psychologists that every idea carries with it the impulse to a bodily movement. Every idea possesses an innate impellent energy.

The mind has been linked to a great switchboard, transforming incoming messages into outgoing ones — sensory stimuli into muscular reactions. The picture is not strictly accurate. The incoming message awakens an impulse to muscular reaction, but whether the reaction shall actually occur or not depends upon other conditions and circumstances.

THE FLOW OF INTELLIGENCE

Yet the fact that every idea is associated with even the impulse to bodily activity, whether the impulse be carried out or not, should, and in fact does, make it possible for us to acquire an understanding of the mental process of attention from a study of the bodily mechanism with which it is so closely involved.

There are countless millions of nerve fibers leading from the surface of the body to the brain. It is along these fibers that messages from the outer world are transmitted to the central intelligence. But in addition to these inbound nerves, there are untold millions of other nerve fibers carrying outbound "currents" to various special centers which directly govern muscular action.

MENTAL ADJUSTMENT

Every impression that you receive from without is therefore something more than merely the result of an incoming current. It is also the starting-point for an outgoing one. Every sense-impression, every idea, carries with it the impulse to some form of bodily action.

Look out of the window. Every separate ray of light falling upon the retina of your eye, and by it transmitted to some brain cell, creates an impulse to move the eye in that direction. Your eye may not move, for the impulse to turn the eye in a number of contrary directions may all be equally strong.

They may balance and offset one another. And in that event your eye must remain stationary.

MENTAL EQUILIBRIUM

On the other hand suppose the impulses from incoming sense-impressions are unequal. The great preponderance of their influence may tend to direct your eye toward a particular spot of vivid color. And yet your eye may not move in that direction. For there may be simultaneously present in your consciousness something besides sense-impressions. There may be an idea with an impellent energy of its own, an idea the innate interest of which demands that the eye shall remain focused upon one supremely interesting spot. Yet all the time those thousands of contrary impulses are working for release, and the position of your eye at any moment is wholly a matter of mental equilibrium.

Every move you make, every step you take, every item, of your outward behavior, the whole sum of your activities in this world, all are the net result of opposing forces.

A multitude of energies are continually at work, struggling to produce certain muscular movements and to restrain antagonistic ones. The complexity of these relations is almost inconceivable.

Nor are you to suppose for a moment that you are aware of all the muscular movements that thus actually come about. Many of these energies find an outlet through the motor nerves and you know neither when nor how. Remember that a smile, a frown, a groan, a sigh, are all just as much the effect of mental impulses as is the act of walking. "A king's breath slays as effectively as an assassin's blow."

Knowing this much of the mechanism of the nervous system of the body, you can now understand how attention does its work.

1. All ideas are but past sense-impressions classified, grouped and catalogued in sub consciousness.

2. Every idea is indissolubly bound up with its appropriate and associated motor impulse.

THE THOUGHT STREAM

3. Whenever any idea becomes active in consciousness, its associated impellent energy tends simultaneously to manifest itself in muscular action. No external action may follow because of the activity at the same time in consciousness of other ideas with impulses to muscular action antagonistic to the first. The stream of the first impulse may be dammed up by contrary impulses, but it is nevertheless there and exerting all its pressure toward release.

4. Thousands of mental images linked with thousands of emotions and impulses must continually arise in your consciousness, but only those have a chance for complete and vivid development that are in harmony with your previous mental disposition. These are the only ones whose impulses are allowed to manifest themselves in outward activity.

THOUGHT MANIFESTATION

5. This mental disposition is determined by your present trend of interest and by your purposive will. Your general interest, your aim in life, determines just what sensory experiences and what ideas shall be selected at any given moment from, the vast stream of incoming sense-impressions and up thronging ideas and shall be allowed to find free expression in outward bodily action.

For example, a composer is engaged in the construction of an opera. In fancy the whole scene is before him. The principals and chorus are in their places. He sees every singer. He has the whole plot in mind. He hears and singles out each one of the multitude of individual tones from the orchestra.

THE MENTAL DISPOSITION

He marks the effect of each individual instrument upon the composite harmony. Suppose that while he is thus absorbed in a creative vision his servant steps to the door and in an ordinary tone of voice informs him that dinner is served. The words will very likely go unheard. The servants message is not in accord with the master's mental disposition. The master's ear receives the empty sound of what the servant says, but it is barred from consciousness. It awakens no perception. And its impulse to appropriate bodily action has no effect, because the master's consciousness is busy with other and different things.

FIXATION OF ATTENTION

6. To fix your attention means to arrange a mental setting or disposition in which the spotlight of your consciousness is reserved for matters related to the subject of attention.

If you fix your attention upon a picture, you examine into its details. In other words, in fixing your attention upon the picture you so arrange the contents of your consciousness as to bring about the bodily action that will increase your knowledge of the picture. Thus, you keep the eye steadfastly turned in that direction. You see every detail in magnified form, and, more important still, antagonistic conscious activities are inhibited so that your mind and judgment are left free for the consideration of the one subject. Thus, attention and fixation of attention is an arrangement of mental forces so that some impulses to action are re-enforced and others are inhibited.

BASIC RULE FOR MENTAL MASTERY

Stop now and mark the significance of all this. You accepted the idea that mental control would mean functional health, material success and happiness, self-realization in the fullest sense. Observe now the basic principle of mind mastery: The mind and all individual human energies are amenable to control by concentration of the attention.

FOCUSING THE MENTAL FORCES

Chapter III

FOCUSING THE MENTAL FORCES

HOW TO MAKE CHARACTER

CONCENTRATION, speaking generally, is defined as "the act of bringing together at one center or focus." Mental concentration is therefore a focusing of the mind upon one object or point.

There is nothing abnormal about the sort of concentration to which we refer. Your individual character or personality is made up simply of the progressive results of your trained habits of concentration of attention. Every conviction that you have on any subject, from religion to politics, is the out-growth of the ways in which you have concentrated your attention.

CONCENTRATION AND CONVICTION

Every conviction thus acquired is wrapped up and stowed away in some thought complex of the past. It is a part of your personality. It will resist, with all the might of its innate energy, the establishment in your mind of any contrary beliefs.

The admonitions of a mother may be so implanted in the mind of her boy that all contrary leanings and impulses will be inhibited. No amount of argument will dispel the faith that religion has fixed in the mind of the true convert. Only the strongest evidence will overcome a man's confidence in the character of an accused friend.

WHAT SELLING EFFECTIVENESS DEPENDS ON

Life is made up of experiences. And the influence of every experience upon your conduct and character depends upon the degree of concentration of attention with which it is received.

And so every idea in memory has a tendency to direct the mind toward those things that are associated with it in time or place or otherwise, and the extent of its influence depends upon its vividness. Every soft inflection in the well-remembered voice of one you love has a tendency to concentrate the activities of your consciousness upon those things that are associated with the object of your affections. Every advertisement, every shop-window display, every prospectus, every business man's artifice, every salesman's lure, depends for its effectiveness upon the extent of its concentrating influence, the extent to which it is able to bring about a concentration of attention in those to whom it is addressed.

THOUGHT ACCEPTANCE AND BELIEF

The mere presence of an idea in consciousness is not concentration. If you suggest to one that a white mist floating across a darkening meadow is a wraith, the idea will be momentarily active in his consciousness, and yet you may have simply succeeded in directing his ordinary attention to an abstract conception. But if he is a believer in spirits and comes away shaken with terror and convinced that he has actually seen a ghost, then there has been a concentration of his consciousness in a scientific sense.

Not every idea presented to consciousness constitutes belief or results in action. In the first instance, the thought of the "ghost" was active in the man's mind, but other conflicting ideas and impulses were simultaneously present denying its reality. In the second instance, however, his consciousness was given over wholly to the idea of a "ghost" that you presented to him. There were present no inhibitory ideas and impulses. He accepted the thought and believed in the reality of it, and, giving free rein to his impulses, he acted accordingly.

Concentration technically interpreted necessarily implies, then, belief in the idea that is the subject of concentration. And this belief releases the impulses for appropriate muscular response.

EFFECTS OF MENTAL CONCENTRATION

How, then, shall we define concentration? Simply thus: Concentration is such a focusing of consciousness upon an idea that if complete it will overcome all conflicting ideas and will result in a belief that will control conduct.

When we say "complete," we mean that the idea in question must hold undisputed sway in consciousness. When this occurs, the idea will be so assimilated as to become incorporated as a part of the personality. You accept it as truth. You believe in it. This belief becomes an element of your personality. It is "your own."

And so it comes about that efficient concentration necessarily results in belief coupled with such, muscular activity as accords with or tends to bring about Uses of the realization of that belief. An over- mastering conviction and an efficient will are therefore the immediate results of complete concentration.

BUSINESS USES OF CONCENTRATION

Concentration will be of value to you in two ways:

1. It will give you a minute and specialized knowledge of things and make you an expert in your line.

It is related of Agassiz that he used to lock a student up in a room day after day with a turtle's head and not release him until he had learned everything there was to know about it. Some achieved this happy result after months of lonely contemplation. Others never did succeed. The successful ones had formed the habit of concentration. They deserved the title of "naturalist" for which Agassiz was fitting them. The unsuccessful ones were forever "blotted from the book of honor and of life."

THOROUGHNESS AS A BUSINESS ASSET

Learn, then, to concentrate, for without it you can pretend to no real knowledge of anything. This is an age of specialists, and the essence of specialization is the acquiring of a minute knowledge of one thing.

Few people realize the immense part that the quality of thoroughness plays in the life of the successful man. The man of millions has generally earned every dollar of his money by doing everything he undertook just a little better than the next man.

The average man is superficial. His motto is, "To seem, not to be." He is willing to "let well enough alone," and has a very modest conception of what "well enough" is. His competitor needs only a little of the leaven of thoroughness to outstrip him.

What you do today is but practice for what you are going to do tomorrow, and if you do whatever you undertake as if your life depended on the issue your capabilities for greater things will grow in proportion.

The fact is that thoroughness is the distinguishing trait of the super-man. And the secret of thoroughness is mental concentration.

THE STREAM THAT FLOWS UP-HILL

II. (And this point is much the more important of the two.) Concentration, whether you will or no, will necessarily result in your driving ahead with all your energy in pursuit of a given end until your point is gained.

The stream of your consciousness is a living current. It is a seething, swirling torrent of activity. Look within and see what is taking place at this moment. You find yourself marking resemblances, noting distinctions, associating one thing with another, and selecting and attending to certain ideas, feeling and impulses while ignoring a multitude of others.

This is the thing called consciousness. It is not an aimless current. It does not flow through the hills and valleys of life adapting itself to the contours of the physical environment. It is a stream that can, if need be, flow up-hill. It is consciousness with a "will." It is consciousness that labors to preserve you, to promote your free development, and to further your practical success.

MENTAL ECONOMY

Make a practice of concentrating upon matters pertaining to a single interest, and you will become absorbed in it as an ideal. You will acquire a standard by which to appraise the value to you of the facts of your life.

Make a practice of concentrating upon a single interest, and you will acquire a constant and completely "possessing" and automatic inhibitory power. You will without thinking refrain from many useless activities. You will refrain from indulgence in pleasures and recreations that would interfere with the accomplishment of your main purpose. You will refrain from wasteful expenditure of your emotions. You will save from a single hour of anger enough energy for a successful day.

THE LEVERS OF INNER CONTROL

Make a practice of concentrating upon a single interest, and you will acquire an ideal that will automatically operate the levers of inner control.

You will acquire a mental machine operating economically, a well-oiled machine that will work automatically, without friction, without effort, almost without thought.

This does not mean that you will be left without the passions that kindle the fires of heroic achievement. Concentration in its highest sense means absorbing, passionate devotion to a cause. It means the state of mind of men whom St. Paul would describe as "fervent" — literally "boiling in spirit."

HOW TO MASS EVERY ATOM
OF ENERGY

Absolute concentration means the massing of every atom of Individual human energy upon a single purpose. It is the acme of efficiency.

Commonly your emotions and desires scatter your energies and exhaust you to no purpose. Organize and concentrate these powers, and the only question remaining unanswered is, "What goal shall I win?"

Be a man of concentration, and you will be a man of purpose, with faith in the attainment of that purpose.

OVERCOMING RESTLESSNESS AND DISCONTENT

Be a man of concentration, and you will possess a mental co-ordination, harmony and unity that will lift you above petty annoyances and free you from such impediments as moods and restlessness and discontent.

Concentrate upon a single purpose. Keep your ideals before you. You cannot then fail to focus all your activities upon the desired end. Only those muscular impulses will find release in actions that are associated with the thought of your desire.

Concentrate upon a single purpose, and you will be possessed of an ideal by which to judge the opportunities of your life. You will shrewdly, naturally and unhesitatingly select those that will contribute to your purpose. You will wisely choose certain pleasures and recreations and discard others. You will have an unerring gauge by which to distinguish luxuries from necessities.

SEEING AND SEIZING OPPORTUNITIES

Concentrate upon a single purpose, and, often when you least expect it, but surely, surely, the time will come when you will see and grasp your chance and strike in with a winning stroke.

This is the law of success. This is what Lincoln really meant, although it may not have occurred to him in just that form, when he said, "I will study and prepare myself and then some day my chance will come."

HOW TO SWAY THE MINDS
OF OTHERS

Would you sway the minds of others? The same principle applies. The man you are to meet is a problem to be solved. Employ the method of Agassiz. Your man has tastes, tendencies, moods, habits and interests that you must consider. He has animosities, determinations, prejudices, inertias and resistances that must be taken into account. Like yourself, he is a living consciousness, a creature of impulses and inhibitions.

Do not try to batter through his inhibitions. Do not employ coercive methods.

Your task is to soothe him into indifference as to all things that tend to inhibit action along desired lines. Do not waste your time in trying to put out of his mind ideas hostile to your purpose.

PRINCIPLES OF PERSUASION

His consciousness is a thing of incessant activity. It must be kept busy. The way to bar out undesirable thought is to fill his mind with other things. Therefore, concentrate his attention upon you and your demands. This done, your cause is gained. You have won the day.

"Your ability to move things," says Waldo P. Warren, "depends largely on where you take hold. I shall never forget the first time I saw the great Ferris wheel — that wonder of two world's fairs. What impressed me most was not its magnitude, but the fact that, in spite of its gigantic size, it required only a comparatively small engine to run it. For unlike most wheels the power was not applied at the center, but at the circumference, thus utilizing the extraordinary leverage of one hundred and eighty feet. The same force, if exerted at the axle, would have been powerless to move the wheel a single inch.

"The lever principle is not confined to mechanical things — it is one of the great fundamental ideas which humanity has discovered.

"When the progress of your campaign is beset with obstacles, whether ignorance, prejudice, injustice, or delay, remember the lever principle. Somewhere there is a move that you can make that will set in motion a chain of events that will eventually move even the greatest obstacle. Don't strain at the hub of the ponderous wheel — move a cog that fits into the rim."

In influencing others just as in mastering yourself, the true test of efficiency, the secret of success, lies in the ability to concentrate the attention.

TWO MORE LAWS FOR SUCCESS-ACHIEVEMENT

Chapter IV

TWO MORE LAWS FOR SUCCESS-ACHIEVEMENT

TWO MORE LAWS FOR SUCCESS-ACHIEVEMENT

MARK now again our seven fundamental principles of Success-Achievement with the addition of certain others now established.

I. All human achievement comes about through some form, of bodily activity.

II. All bodily activity is caused, controlled and directed by the mind.

III. The mind is the instrument that we must employ in the accomplishment of any purpose.

IV. You have but one mind, but it is a mind with phases of consciousness and phases of sub consciousness.

V. Your consciousness is made up in part of present sensory experiences and in part of complexes drawn from sub consciousness.

VI. Your sub consciousness is a reservoir of classified complexes made up of ideas, emotions and motor impulses.

VII. The presence of any idea in your consciousness tends simultaneously to produce an associated "feeling" and to impel you to certain appropriate muscular activities.

VIII. The attention determines what ideas, emotions and motor impulses shall be active in consciousness.

IX. Concentrate the attention and you automatically control and direct all bodily activities.

THE ART OF CONCENTRATION

Chapter V

THE ART OF CONCENTRATION

WORLD BUILDERS AND CONCENTRATION

AH, BUT how to concentrate!" you may say. "So far from being able to concentrate the attention of others, I have never been able to do any concentrating of my own."

Be patient, friend. You shall learn the art of concentration. There are methods and devices that if faithfully employed put this power within reach of everyone. But first you must realize the wide reach of this mighty weapon. You must know something of the processes and principles underlying its scientific use.

We want you to approach these great truths in a spirit of reverence and awe; this not alone because of their intrinsic worth, but also because of their influence in molding the history of men. For the world owes all that is great in religion, in war, in art, in science, in all noble endeavor, to concentration, the concentration of divine talents with unswerving faith upon a lofty purpose.

It was concentration that made Alexander master of the world, sighing for more worlds to conquer. It was concentration that made Buddha the Light of Asia, that made Confucius devote his life through incalculable suffering to great teachings, and made Socrates prefer the cup of hemlock to the repudiation of his principles, it created Zoroaster, farther back than memory. It created Mohammed, the prophet of Arabia. And with its unwavering light came the Founder of Christianity, the Nazarene.

Here in America, it was concentration that gave us Washington, that inspired Lincoln. It was concentration that built the first steamboat, that invented the cotton gin, that discovered the secret of telegraphy, that made Edison the "wizard of electricity." It was concentration that lifted Rockefeller and Morgan to the pinnacles of opulent power. It was concentration, nation-wide, and based upon an enduring faith, that preserved our national integrity through the scourging fire of internecine strife.

PRACTICE OF THE OCCULT

In none of these instances was there any deliberate concentration of mental forces. The vast and overpowering desire was in each case brought about by other influences than the action of the individual will.

Yet the study and practice of deliberate concentration, of voluntary concentration, of concentration as an art, is no new thing. In various guises it has appeared upon the stage of history among all races and nations and in all times since the world was young.

The practice of concentration as an art has heretofore always been shrouded in occultism and mystery. This is because its devotees have had merely an empirical knowledge of the subject. They have observed what could be accomplished by concentrative devices and methods, but they have had no comprehension of the reason for the results they observed. Standing back in astonishment at the wonders they were able to work, and unable to explain these occurrences in any rational way, they have ascribed the results to miraculous or supernatural agencies.

METHODS OF APPEAL

In all ages and in all climes, man has bowed before an Intelligent Power capable of producing or healing diseases in the human body and capable of bestowing or withholding peace and plenty. The character of this unseen and intangible Force has varied with different races of men and different periods of their history. But always and everywhere we find the startling fact that all the peoples of the earth, civilized and uncivilized, have used, and still do use, generically, the same methods of appealing to this invisible Power.

PRIEST, MAGI, FAKIR, YOGI

The Chaldean seer gazed into the eye of a glittering gem until a trance ensued in which he could divine the purposes of the Mighty. So did the Egyptian priest, the Persian magi, and the Hindu fakir, all of whom still bring themselves to a trance-like state by fixation of gaze. That strange sect of early Christians known as Tasko-drugites accomplished the same results during prayer by looking fixedly at the forefinger held close before the face and pointing at the nose. The monks of the Greek Church in the convent of Mount Athos sought freedom from the distractions of a noisy world and entered into communion with the Holy Spirit by gazing steadily at their umbilicus. The fetich worshiper fixes his fascinated eye upon a stick or stone in which dwells for him all Power and Beneficence. The Annamite gazes with wondering trust at two burning sticks fastened behind the left ear of the magician who slowly and impressively revolves upon his heel.

Charms and idolatrous ceremonies, occult "mysteries" and religious practices, witches' incantations and priestly sacrifices, hideous noises and diabolical make-up of "medicine man" and "voodoo doctor " all are but ways and means devised by men to thwart the efforts of evil spirits and conciliate the good.

THE CALCIUM-LIGHT OF INTEREST

And all have two elements in common. First, they serve to grip the interest of the faith-full one. Second, having focused his attention, they then direct it toward belief in the realization of a hope; they play it like a calcium light upon the consummation so devoutly wished.

All are but different devices for bringing about that mental concentration which we have defined as the overmastering focusing of consciousness upon the belief in an idea.

HINDU "YOGA"

The prayer of pious persons, the "Yoga" of the Hindu, the "silence" of the disciple of "New Thought," the meditation of the philosopher, all find their elements of efficacious truth in this basic principle. From the routine telling of beads of orthodox Christians to the "disembodied" soul of the Hindu "adept," all are but manifestations and degrees of mental concentration.

Consider the occultism of the Hindu now in such vogue. "Yoga," literally; — translated, means "concentration." It is used symbolically by the Hindu mystic to signify concentration or union with a Supreme Being. According to the fourth chapter of the Bhagavad Gita, many "adepts," in order to be entirely freed from the distraction of bodily sensations, even "sacrifice the sense of hearing and the other senses in the fires of restraint." Others "by abstaining from food, sacrifice life in their life."

DEMONSTRABLE THUTHS VS.
MYSTIC FORMULAS

There is no difference in principle between these practices and the self-flagellations of the early monks, the Master's forty-day fast in the wilderness, and the asceticism of Simeon Stylites, who passed his life on top of a pillar. All these procedures must be looked upon as devices intended to facilitate mental concentration.

Think, now, of the advantage that you possess over other exponents of the art of concentration. You have learned the exact truth in regard to mental operations and processes. You have taken a vast amount of pains in doing so. But now that it comes time for you to apply these principles by devising easy ways for practicing concentration with a view to attaining specific results, you do not have to go groping about in the darkness of occultism and mystery.

THE FAITH THAT KNOWS

You know the elements with which you have to deal.

You know them as realities, as demonstrable truths of modern science.

And when you come to make use of these devices you will not question their efficacy. You will have no doubts as to your success. You will be inspired with the faith that is born of knowledge, as distinguished from the faith that is artificially created by mystic formulas and priestly authority.

The faith that knows was the faith of the Son of God. Jesus knew the power of the human spirit. He knew how to heal the sick, how to feed the multitude with but a single loaf, how to confer the peace "that passeth understanding." This was the secret of his perfect power.

Yet even Jesus required certain conditions for the "demonstration" of his powers. Even Jesus was unable to perform miracles among the people of Nazareth because of their "unbelief." And it was Jesus who, when he had healed a certain sick man, uttered these words of deep scientific significance — "Thy faith hath made thee whole."

Faith, belief in the attainment of a desired end, is as essential to success scientifically sought as sought in any other way, because, as you have seen, it sets in motion actual forces.

SUCCESS SCIENTIFICALLY SOUGHT

But scientific method possesses four exclusive advantages. First, the faith it demands is a faith that all may acquire, because it is a faith that reasoning will create, not destroy; second, it is a faith that is perfect, because based on judgment; third, it is a faith that is lasting because truth is immutable; fourth, it is a faith that you may deliberately and scientifically acquire, because you now know that faith in a given idea means nothing more nor less than the dominance of that idea in consciousness.

So, then, you can achieve nothing without faith — faith in the ideals on which your attention dwells.

And through faith and ideals, and your consecration of them, and your concentration upon them, lies the way for you to acquire inner control, to escape wasteful moods and emotions, to master your energies, to become efficient in the highest sense and to the last degree.

HYPNOTISM AS ILLUSTRATING THE POWER OF MENTAL CONCENTRATION

Chapter VI

HYPNOTISM AS ILLUSTRATING THE POWER OF MENTAL CONCENTRATION

POPULAR IGNORANCE CONCERNING HYPNOTISM

HERE is one field which seems especially designed to illustrate the operation of the principle of mental control. It is a state of consciousness in which problems may be made and solved as if to order.

This state is hypnosis.

Hypnotism and hypnosis are topics concerning which the general public entertains delusions that are astonishingly numerous, extraordinary and at the same time inexcusable.

No class or condition of men has a monopoly of ignorance on this subject. It is not confined to the illiterate. Newspapers and magazines, even court proceedings, abound in references to hypnotism and hypnosis that are not merely inaccurate; they are grotesque.

The cause of these misconceptions may doubtless be traced in part to the surprising character of the phenomena themselves and in part to the original sources of our knowledge of these phenomena, which from the beginning have been under the prostituting influence of the charlatan and the mountebank.

HISTORY OF HYPNOTISM

The study of hypnotism must be said to have had its origin in the observations of Mesmer, for while, as an art, it has under various names been practiced by the sages of the East since time out of mind, yet it did not come under the analytical eye of Western civilization until within the last hundred years.

Mesmer was essentially unscientific. He unquestionably practiced hypnotism, aroused interest in the subject and gave to the world much valuable data; but instead of investigating his facts in a rational way he undertook to explain them by magical and miraculous agencies.

His assumption that the hypnotic influence was due to "fluidic emanations" from the operator to the patient was, at least in his day, nothing more nor less than an appeal to the "supernatural."

The general public has never got much beyond Mesmer's conception of weird power on the part of the operator, a conception fostered by the unscientific men of his time and kept alive in our day by the disgraceful shams of stage hypnotism.

If scientists had investigated these mental phenomena as promptly and thoroughly as they have taken up the physical facts of sound, magnetism and electricity, the public judgment in regard to hypnotism would have been intelligently directed, just as it has been in regard to electricity and electrical phenomena. Unfortunately the use made of hypnotism in the early days was such as to disgust men of scientific attainments and to surround the subject in the popular mind with an aura of magic that envelops it to this day.

MESMERISM, MAGIC
AND DOCTOR BRAID

It was Dr. James Braid, of Manchester, England, whose clear insight and painstaking labors first caused men of science to look upon hypnotic phenomena with respectful interest.

After the French Academy of Science had decided that the claims of the Mesmerists were unworthy of investigation. Braid undertook a careful study of the subject.

He proved that hypnosis was not the effect of any force transmitted from operator to subject, but was brought about by "suggestion."

He demonstrated that the cause was not external to the subject, but was a mental "setting or attitude" induced by the operator in the subject's own mind.

He rejected the term "mesmerism," so long associated with ideas of magic, and substituted the term hypnosis, derived from the Greek word for sleep.

In the main, Braid's conception of hypnosis, after enduring vicissitudes of rejection, neglect and doubt, has come to be generally adopted in the world of thought.

The popular idea of hypnosis, as something mystical, involving an uncanny influence on the part of the operator, is not unnatural. To have a few softly spoken words or a few passes over a man's face result in his passive acceptance of utter absurdities as if they were inspired truths, is certainly disconcerting.

WEIRD EFFECTS OF HYPNOTISM

Ordinarily, it takes either force or persuasion by one man to bring about action or belief on the part of another.

Man is a rational being, and his normal actions and beliefs are the result of reflection and judgment.

When hypnotized, however, he acts without reflection. He sees with the eyes of another, and he passively accepts that other's judgment. His movements, even his thoughts, are directed by another, with seemingly mechanical control.

What more natural, therefore, than that the unenlightened should regard the hypnotist as possessed of occult power, and the subject as entirely at the mercy of the operator's will?

EIGHT COMMON DELUSIONS
CONCERNING HYPNOTISM

Here is an enumeration of some of the many popular delusions on this subject of hypnotism, to each of which we append a statement of the facts:

1. It is the general belief that the subject must lose consciousness when hypnotized. The fact is that in most cases the subject remains perfectly conscious. Brilliant practical results are achieved with subjects who scarcely become drowsy.

2. The belief prevails that only the weak-minded, or at least the weak-willed, can be effectually hypnotized. The truth is that persons of understanding and healthy independence of will, capable of intelligent co-operation, make the best subjects, while children, hysterics and insane persons are almost impossible.

3. It is a current opinion that the persons who can be hypnotized are comparatively few. As a matter of fact, the great majority of people can be hypnotized to an extent quite sufficient for the accomplishment of practical results.

4. Another wide-spread and mistaken notion is that the hypnotizer must be naturally endowed with some strange aptitude for influencing others. The only grain of truth in this is that intelligence, assurance, earnestness and an

engaging address make for success in this field of endeavor as in any other.

5. Hypnosis is commonly ascribed to subtle emanations passing from operator to subject. The real explanation is the suggestion of a belief to a super concentrated attention.

That the hypnotic state, or hypnosis, as it is called, results from the action of the subject's own mind, and not from "magnetic" or "fluidic" emanations or any other external agency, is proved by a much-quoted experiment of Braid's.

One of Mesmer's followers had claimed that he could bring about the hypnotic "trance" without the knowledge or consent of the subject. Braid did not believe this possible. To determine the question, he induced the mesmerist to visit him at his house. He then brought to the house the subject with whom the mesmerist had been though the subject knew nothing of the mesmerist's presence in the house. The subject sat a few feet from the mesmerist in another room with the door between slightly ajar. The mesmerist worked nearly an hour to induce hypnosis. His efforts were without any apparent effect. The subject was then informed of the presence of the mesmerist and of his efforts to I hypnotize him. Immediately the subject went into the mesmeric sleep, thereby proving that his own mind was the chief instrument in the result.

Indeed, the operator is not even an absolutely essential factor in the induction of hypnosis. This is sufficiently proved by the phenomena of somnambulism, which is recognized as a form of hypnosis, and also by the fact that many persons have actually succeeded in deliberately hypnotizing themselves.

6. Most persons believe that in the hands of an unscrupulous person hypnotism may be used as an instrument for the commission of crime. All authorities on hypnotism are agreed, however, that to bring about the actual commission of an act offensive to the moral sense of the subject is practically impossible. The suggestion of such an act is either ignored by the subject or results in the subject's being immediately aroused.

Hypnosis is not produced by any miracle-working genius, but by the action of the subject's own mind.

Therefore, no man can be hypnotized without his consent.

Instances may occur, particularly after long practice in hypnosis, where the subject's consent seems to be lacking, but it must be borne in mind that the consent need not be a formal expression of the will. It may simply be an acquiescent consciousness of the fact that the operator is thinking of the desired result.

7. Another popular fallacy is that the frequent repetition of hypnosis will weaken or enslave the patient's will. The only reported instances of this kind have resulted from reckless and incessant practice of hypnotism for theatrical purposes, when the subject has been called upon for hire to act the part of a human bridge, a pincushion or a buffoon.

The cases of reported injury are few and complicated and difficult of determination. In any event, it is not the hypnosis itself, but the harmful character of the belief implanted during the hypnosis, that must be held responsible. Doubtless whatever is capable of use is capable also of abuse. Certain it is that contrary effects are possible, that diseases of immorality may be cured and the moral stamina increased and the will strengthened by appropriate ideas presented to the subject's mind during hypnosis.

8. Another delusion, prevalent fortunately only among the illiterate, seems to be that any compelling influence of one person over another, whereby the latter appears dependent on the other's will, is hypnotism. We often run across the assertion, particularly in newspaper accounts of lurid matters, when speaking of any person who has apparently been dominated by another, that he was "hypnotized." Such loose talk as this reveals a total misconception of hypnotism and hypnosis.

HOW TO HYPNOTIZE

Chapter VII

HOW TO HYPNOTIZE

HOW TO HYPNOTIZE

THE usual procedure used in inducing hypnosis, as set forth by a well-known writer on the subject, is about as follows:

"After talking sympathetically with the subject, sometimes for an hour or two, in regard to the failing he wishes removed, thoroughly acquainting myself with his dominant propensities or controlling thoughts, and, above all, securing his confidence, I ask him to assume a comfortable reclining position on a lounge, and then continue a soothing conversation along lines like the following with a view to producing a monotonous impression on eye and ear:

"'I wish you would look at this diamond [or select any convenient object in line of vision] in a dreamy, listless manner, with a blank expressionless stare, thinking of nothing, not concentrating your mind or focusing your eye upon it, but relaxing the ocular muscles so that it has a confused outline. Abstain from that effort with the eyes that you are accustomed to make in order to see a near object distinctly. Rather look through the stone and past it, as you look at a dead tree standing between you and a distant view you are contemplating."

"Make no effort, for there is nothing you can do to encourage the approach of the favorable mind state. Do not wonder what is going to happen, for nothing is going to happen. Do not be apprehensive, or suspicious, or distrustful. Do not desire that anything shall take place, nor watch to see what may occur — nor seek to analyze what is going on in your mind. You are as negative, indolent, and indifferent as you can be without trying to be."

"You are to expect the familiar signs of the approach of sleep, and they are all associated with the failure of the senses and the standstill of the brain — heavy eyelids, reluctant ears, muscles and skin indifferent to stimuli of temperature, humidity, penetrability, etc."

Already that delightful sensation of drowsiness "weighs your eyelids down and steeps your senses in forgetfulness," and you yield to the impulse as the curtains are dropped between you and the outside world of color and light. And your ear seeks to share in this rest of the senses.

As darkness is the sleep of the eye, so is silence that of the ear; and your ear secures silence by deadening itself to sound impressions. The sounds of my voice lose interest for you, and force and decisiveness, and seem to be receding into a mysterious remoteness, whither you are disinclined to follow them, leaving you in a state of delightful relaxation. A grateful sense of surrender to some pleasing influence which you cannot resist, and would not if you could, descends upon you and enwraps your whole body in its beneficent embrace, and you are physically happy. Refreshing sleep has come to you.'"

This process may take a minute or two, or it may occupy half an hour, but when it is completed the subject is ready for the appropriate practical suggestions.

The suggestions are made as emphatically as possible. They are presented in as many different ways as possible. They are repeated plainly and insistently. They are exaggerated, on the principle that the marksman must aim high. Thus, in a case of insomnia, it may be suggested that the sufferer will sleep twelve hours the following night, although eight would certainly suffice.

When the suggestions are concluded, the subject is allowed to rest for a time and is then told that he may awaken. If no such permission were given, he would gradually rouse himself, just as if he were waking from ordinary sleep.

MODERN PRACTICAL USES OF HYPNOTISM

Chapter VIII

MODERN PRACTICAL USES OF HYPNOTISM

MODERN PRACTICAL USES OF HYPNOTISM

THERE is scarcely any strictly functional derangement of mind or body, from neuralgia, paralysis and diabetes to alcoholism, kleptomania and moral perversions, that has not yielded to treatment by hypnotic suggestion.

Every kind of innate mental aptitude, such, for example, as the talent for public speaking, for music, painting and literature, has also been aided and stimulated to expression by this means.

Advanced scientific men have employed it and are today employing it in countless ways for the improvement of the mental and physical well-being of their patients, and its value and importance are recognized today in the medical and psychological departments of all great universities.

It must be confessed that this friendly attitude of scientific medical men toward the study and practice of hypnotism is a matter of very recent years. The earlier exponents of the subject among physicians were mostly ignored by their medical brethren or were openly denounced as impostors.

Many reasons conspired to bring this about. One was the disparaging attitude of the patient himself, who could hardly be expected to realize at once the vast resources of energy and power stored within so familiar a part of himself as his own mind.

Another may possibly have been a spirit of commercialism that saw in the new methods a vastly increased efficiency of the individual and a corresponding decline in the business of the prescriber of medicines.

A third reason was the fact that the new science had first to be taught in the medical schools and to revolutionize their methods before it could hope to be accepted by the great body of physicians, with many of whom their graduation from the medical school marked the end of their delving into first principles.

Yet all the literature of medicine, whether of ancient or modern times, abounds in illustrations of the power of the mind over the body in health and in disease. And medical science has always, though perhaps unconsciously, based much of its practice on this principle. No reputable school of medicine ever failed to instruct its students in practical applications of the principle of mental influence at the bedside of their patients. A brisk and cheery manner, a hopeful countenance, a supremely assured and confident demeanor — these things have always been regarded by the medical profession as but second in importance to sanitation and material remedies; while the value of the sugar-coated bread pill when the diagnosis was uncertain, has long been recognized.

The properly trained nurse has always been expected to supplement the efforts of the attending physician by summoning the mental forces of the patient to his aid. She, therefore, surrounds the patient with an atmosphere of comfortable assurance. And by constantly advising him of his satisfactory progress toward speedy recovery she seeks to instil hope, confidence and mental effort.

To quote Dr. Didama, "The ideal physician irradiates the sick chamber; with the light of his cheerful presence. He may not be hilarious — he is not indifferent — but he has an irrepressible good-nature which lifts the patient out of the slough of despond and places his feet on the firm land of health. In desperate cases, even a little harmless levity may be beneficial. A well-timed jest may break up a congestion; a pun may add pungency to the sharpest stimulant." Dr. Oliver Wendell Holmes reduced this principle to its cash equivalent when he said that a cheerful smile might be worth five thousand dollars a year to a physician. Today, psychotherapy, or the healing of bodily disease by mental influence, has the unqualified endorsement of the American Therapeutic Society, the only national organization in America devoted exclusively to therapeutics. It has the enthusiastic support of men of such recognized international leadership in the scientific world and in the medical profession as Freud, Jeung, Bleuler, Breuer, Prince, Janet, Babinski, Putnam, Gerrish, Sidis, Dubois, Miinsterberg, Jones, Brill, Donley, Waterman and Taylor. A vast array of specific cases of the successful employment of hypnotic suggestion for the cure of functional diseases or for the development of latent mental powers and abilities may be found in the published works of these men.

The present attitude of reputable science toward the principle that the mind controls all bodily operations is, then, one of positive conviction. The world's foremost thinkers accept its truth. The interest of enlightened men and women everywhere is directed toward the mind as a powerful curative force and as a regenerative influence of hitherto undreamed-of resource.

Bear in mind this is not intended as a practical study of hypnosis. The value of the subject for us lies in its illustration of the possibilities of mental control and in its indication of how that control may be achieved.

The remedial effects of hypnotic suggestion are so startling, so like magic, that it is no wonder the popular mind looks upon hypnotizing as a phenomenon bordering on the miraculous. To pass one's hands for a few moments in front of a man's face, and then banish a severe pain or cure serious illness by mere words is to apparently violate all natural laws of cause and effect. The untutored observer sees no limit to the possibilities of such an agency and classes it with the practice of the "black art."

SCIENTIFIC EXPLANATION OF HYPNOTISM

Chapter IX

SCIENTIFIC EXPLANATION OF HYPNOTISM

MENTAL EQUILIBRIUM AND POWERS OF RESISTANCE

WHAT is hypnosis? We cannot go far astray if we define it as a condition outwardly resembling sleep and characterized by extreme credulousness.

We have already studied concentration in its relation to normal states of mind and have learned that the effect upon consciousness of a suggested belief depends upon the degree of concentration of the consciousness to which it is presented. In other words, that the extent of the influence of a proffered suggestion depends upon the degree of equilibrium, as to impulses and inhibitions, of the consciousness to which the suggestion is addressed.

Now, no new principle is involved in hypnotism. The most startling effects of hypnotic suggestion are not due to any special power flowing from mind to mind, but to a change of equilibrium of the subject's own mind.

All that is needed to prepare the soil for the accomplishment of this change is the induction of a degree of credulousness greater than the normal. The mind in a state of abnormal credulousness will accept and believe any ideas that are proffered to it, even ideas that are contradicted by the plain testimony of the senses.

Let us experiment. By a few minutes' talk, coupled with the voluntary composure of the subject, we bring him into a deep hypnotic trance. He is now unable to resist any suggestion we may make that does not positively violate his standards of morality. Whether the suggestion is one arousing an impulse to inhibit an action, as "You will not lift your foot," or one instilling a belief that necessarily inhibits an action, as "You cannot lift your foot," the effect is the same; the foot is glued to the floor. If we tell him that his friend has left the room, he will neither see that friend nor hear any word that the friend may utter, and a hat placed on the friend's head will seem to hang in mid-air. Every sense-impression not in accord with our suggestions is inhibited and shifted into sub consciousness without having been consciously perceived. The process is the same as that during sleep, when for the mother all sound impressions are inhibited except those from her restless child.

What has happened to our subject? Were the empty words we uttered sufficient in themselves, like a mystic formula, to bring about the change?

CONTROLLING SUBJECTS
AT A DISTANCE

By no means. I might have produced the same effect by a few monotonous passes with the hands, or by requiring the subject to gaze at my finger held close before his eyes. It is possible for me to have hypnotized him automatically, as it were, my thoughts being actually otherwise engaged. I might have used one of the various devices of revolving mirrors to focus his attention, thus eliminating my own personality as a factor in the process. I might even in some cases have merely sent him a letter advising him that two minutes after reading it he would fall into the hypnotic sleep; and under certain conditions the phenomenon would have occurred, even though in the mean time I had been removed by death from the possibility of exerting a personal influence.

Obviously, then, hypnotism is not necessarily the result of any special energy, like magnetism, or even of an exercise of the operator's will. No special qualifications are required. Almost any intelligent person can hypnotize or be hypnotized.

HYPNOSIS DISTINGUISHED FROM NATURAL SLEEP

How is so strange a mental transformation to be accounted for?

We might compare it to sleep. But can that be sleep in which the mind is unusually quick in its associative imagery and in which the causal judgments are faultlessly correct? If I tell our subject that he is standing in a canon of the Colorado Rockies, he sees glaciers and snowy mountains, tumbling waterfalls and rocky gorges. These things are pictured, not in the distorted form of dreams, but vividly, truthfully. His mind is awake; but thoughts and impulses in conflict with my suggestion are inhibited.

To be sure, the easiest method of inducing hypnosis is to suggest to the subject the belief that he is falling asleep. This is because such a belief tends to inhibit all ideas, all consciousness, leaving the mind a blank page to receive the suggestions of the operator.

But natural sleep is marked by a comparative torpidity of the senses and a diminution of discriminatory power, while hypnosis is characterized by an, increased sensitiveness and a quickened memory in the field suggested by the operator.

In this field sense-impressions are perceived that would pass unnoticed by the normal consciousness, and memories long forgotten and inaccessible are brought forth.

THE MENTAL PROCESS THAT EXPLAINS HYPNOTISM

The Mental Besides all this, the profound or somnambulic state of hypnosis shades off into countless transitional or so called "hypnoidal" states in which the readiness to believe remains, but in which the resemblances to sleep are scarcely discernible.

For the explanation of hypnosis we must refer to the process of attention.

We have elsewhere observed that inhibition is an essential element of every act of attention. Everything not related to the subject attended to is inhibited, while a great number of sense-impressions, ideas and complexes that are so related can be simultaneously active in consciousness. The inhibition rests only on those complexes requiring a contrary mental attitude.

The hypnotic state is marked by an abnormal increase in selective and inhibitory power. The sense organs of Hypnotism the hypnotic, just as in a normal state, positively shout aloud the fact that his friend is standing before him, but they are powerless before a discriminating attention so controlled that it may allow his consciousness to perceive nothing but the friend's hat.

In fact, hypnosis is nothing more nor less than a state of "over-attention" Attention under normal circumstances means only special distinctness of the object attended to; "over-attention" in hypnosis means unquestioning faith in all that comes from the object attended to — that is to say, the operator.

The mechanical passes, the staring eye, the monotonous speech, the thoughts of sleep, the tired feeling, all withdraw attention from all other things and fasten it upon the one absorbing idea of the hypnotizer. All that the hypnotizer says and does is seized upon with avidity, and absorbed with blind acceptance. The subject is told that he cannot speak, and the motor impulses necessary to speech are inhibited. What can he do but surrender helplessly to life as a mute? The suggestional influence operates automatically.

Hypnosis, then, is a state of "over-attention," or, in the phrase we have adopted, a state of mental concentration.

THE STATE OF ABNORMAL CONCENTRATION

And the results of mental concentration when thus exhibited overwhelm us with wonder unless we are careful to remember the infinite complexity of the mental apparatus.

If we lose sight of this complexity and wide-reaching power of the mind, we are apt to feel, in considering hypnotism, as if one person had exerted a mysterious influence over the other, as if the will of one had in some uncanny fashion mastered the will of the other.

As soon, however, as we realize that physical health and functional disturbance, belief and action, judgment and conduct, happiness and despair, are all the result of the co-operation of a vast number of mental forces, which have had to overcome and inhibit conflicting mental forces, when we realize that every one of these results is the outcome of an overbalancing of this complex mechanism, then we understand how it is possible for deliberately directed influences from without or from within to help one side or the other to preponderance.

With these explanations and illustrations of the powers and practical uses of an abnormal degree of mental concentration, and how this condition can be deliberately brought about by devices that lull the mind into a condition of receptivity, as it is employed by eminent psychologists and psychotherapists under the name of "hypnotism," the student must be well fortified in the essential principles of mental control.

He is now fitted to appreciate, understand and make use of practical instructions. Succeeding books will therefore be devoted to methods and directions for the attainment of success by scientific psychological practices.